# To Jeffrey with Love
## A Heartwarming Story of a Mother and her Special Needs Son

### ALYCE MORRIS WINSTON

To Jeffrey with Love
A Heartwarming Story of a Mother and her Special Needs Son
All Rights Reserved.
Copyright © 2019 Alyce Morris Winston
v4.0

The opinions expressed in this manuscript are solely the opinions of the author and do not represent the opinions or thoughts of the publisher. The author has represented and warranted full ownership and/or legal right to publish all the materials in this book.

This book may not be reproduced, transmitted, or stored in whole or in part by any means, including graphic, electronic, or mechanical without the express written consent of the publisher except in the case of brief quotations embodied in critical articles and reviews.

The Jeffrey Foundation Press

ISBN: 978-0-578-22241-7

Cover & interior images by Alyce Morris Winston.

PRINTED IN THE UNITED STATES OF AMERICA

## PRAISE FOR ALYCE MORRIS WINSTON
## & THE JEFFREY FOUNDATION

"A guiding light from above directs Alyce in all she does to benefit (her children). She is unique, and we appreciate and love her."

—Helen and Peter Mark Richman

"Once in a while, a foundation comes along that meets the needs of the special needs children and their families in our community. I have watched The Jeffrey Foundation grow through the years and commend Ms. Alyce Morris Winston and her staff and volunteers for all their dedicated service to the community for over forty-seven years."

—Honorable Diane Watson

"A fabulous, quintessential woman who has made the world a better place is my longtime friend, Alyce Morris Winston."

—Connie Stevens

"I have been a strong supporter of The Jeffrey Foundation since my son Brian was in The Jeffrey Foundation's after-school program, Saturday Fun Club, and Jeffrey Boy Scout troop. It is remarkable what Alyce and her team have accomplished and how many children and families the programs have served in forty-seven years!

—Marcia Brickley
*Vice Chair of The Jeffrey Foundation Board of Directors*

"You have grown our dream into something much larger than I could have ever expected since the time my brother David attended. I thank you from the bottom of my heart for being there for my family when we needed you most."

—Melissa Thompson

"I commend Jeffrey's mother for having forged ahead in sometimes trying times, and I hope she will continue to receive the support needed to provide these programs. Most of the children served come from single-parent families. These are vital programs and I'm pleased to recommend them to parents, as well as encourage community support."

—Victor A. Signorelli
*Director of Special Schools, Los Angeles Unified School District*

# Acknowledgments

I want to thank all my friends, staff, supporters, board members, and donors for their many years of service and support of the Jeffrey Foundation. I feel so fortunate to have been able to see my son Jeffrey enjoy the quality of life he so deserved, and now, every day, I see the Foundation children enjoying quality childcare and educational programs they so deserve. My heart is also full when I witness how the parents of these special needs children are finding comfort, and a home, with the Jeffrey Foundation for the support that they need—not only for their children but so they can provide for their families. The Foundation's Circle of Love has also contributed so much throughout the years, and they continue to support and cheerlead all our programs and help us meet our goals. I cannot tell you how blessed I feel that the Foundation staff and volunteers are carrying the torch into the future. I especially thank the board for their support and care over the years, as well as putting us in touch with the proper people and donors that keep our forty-seven-year-old agency in the community, helping keep Special Needs and low-income children's programs going, year after year! I could not have done it alone!

Alyce Morris Winston

*To Jeffrey*

I dreamed we walked together, you and me.
Not I beside your wheelchair as it were.
Your tall shadow moved just ahead of mine,
As we made our way to work for our just cause.

To those who needed us, we have surely come.
For our love and assistance, we can share.
It is ever thus, even though you are gone,
I know you are always in God's care.

We care for those afflicted and undone,
For those who cannot see or walk or trust.
Your love and faith still lead us, oh my son,
And because of you, I have the strength to carry on.


Alyce Morris Winston

# Foreword

The world could use a few more people like Alyce Morris Winston - a no-nonsense, bold, strong, fearless woman with unwavering patience and a wonderful attitude.

Being the single mother of a child with muscular dystrophy in 1972 was quite a daunting hurdle. After an exhausting search for help for her son Jeffrey, and after realizing there were no options, Alyce took matters into her own hands and formed her own organization.

Starting in her living room with no money, Alyce used the only things she had to achieve her goal: persistence, courage, faith, and love. Over the last 48 years, the Jeffrey Foundation has been her life's mission, and today it is one of the most successful children's charities in the world, helping countless special needs children.

I remember the night we met Alyce in 1998 at a charity event at which I was the emcee. She came right up to my wife Helen and me and announced that I was going to be the emcee at her next event. Without knowing any details of who she was or of her organization, I accepted! That's the kind of persuasive woman she can be. That invitation began a long-standing friendship and a 25-year working relationship with Alyce and the Jeffrey Foundation that is still going strong today.

Whenever Alyce has reached out, it has been an honor and a privilege for my wife and me to assist in any capacity we can. When Steve Allen, the previous chairman of the Celebrity Committee, passed away in 2000, Alyce again came to me and asked if I would be willing to take over the position.

My wife and I were happy to oblige. As Steve Allen and his lovely wife Jayne Meadows did before us, we tapped our personal resources and enlisted the help of some of our good friends in the industry. When they would come to the Foundation's facilities and see how a better quality of life was being created for all Alyce's precious special needs children, they all jumped at the chance to come on board.

Alyce has continued to work tirelessly, both as a hands-on worker with all the Foundation children and as an extraordinary hostess for all the Foundation's fund-raising social events. She and her husband Edgar have led an exemplary life helping others. My wife and I are pleased and grateful to call her a good friend.

"To Jeffrey with Love" allows the reader to see Alyce's world through the eyes of hundreds of children who have looked up to her through tears of gratitude.

-Peter Mark and Helen Richman

# CHAPTER I

Tomahawk, Wisconsin, was my birthplace. Dad was a young orchestra leader, paper mill worker, and sometimes a shoe clerk. Mother was a teacher, trained at the local normal school in Merrill, Wisconsin, which is around twenty or thirty miles south of Tomahawk.

I appeared at birth on May 4, 1930, and according to all present, I was born in a veil and had black hair covering parts of my face and lots of hair on my head.

My father, Ray Davis, was born in Terre Haute, Indiana, and had come up to Wisconsin playing in a resort in upper Wisconsin, where my mother had met him. She was a dancer; she had taken a break from college, I guess and gone up to do this show at a resort. That's where they met.

So much for that . . . back to my birth. I was a big baby—almost nine pounds. I was raised with a lot of uncles and aunts and grandparents on my mother's side, as there was a divorce when I was a little over a year old.

# TO JEFFREY WITH LOVE

Mom got tired of following Dad on his gigs with the Gabe Davis Band all over Wisconsin and Illinois and came home to her mom and dad in Tomahawk.

My early life was spent happily at Grandma Damon's house. I started kindergarten at four and Mom got married when I was three, to Leonard Storm, whom she had met at a local dance.

We moved to Milwaukee when I was in first grade. I went to Wisconsin Avenue School, in Milwaukee.

In 1939, Leonard, my stepfather, who was a carpenter, took mom and me on the road with our sleeping trailer, which he had built, and went to California, where he looked for work as a carpenter.

Along the way on Route 66, we stopped and saw many interesting sites. Finally, we arrived in Los Angeles in late fall 1941, and I remember my first view of the Pacific Ocean in Santa Monica.

Once settled in LA, because I tested too high for elementary school, even though I was only eleven years old, I started school at Thomas Starr King Junior High.

Besides my introduction to Los Angeles, we started going to church at the Angeles Temple, which was started by Aimee Semple McPherson, the famous evangelist. My mother was very ill with lung disease and other ailments, and she was prayed for in the healing service at the 500 Room, and was healed by divine healing!

# CHAPTER I

My mother was on eleven medications on our trip out to Los Angeles from Milwaukee. So, when she no longer had to take them anymore, her healing was a great moment in all of our lives. Afterward, she didn't have to take any medications and was free of all her ailments! It was indeed an answer to our prayers!

Mother's healing also set us on a path of faith, and mother soon enrolled in the Bible College L.I.F.E. in Los Angeles, which was founded by Aimee Semple McPherson, the famous evangelist and missionary.

Mother soon showed a great interest in becoming a missionary to China and encouraged me to follow that path as well.

I became a child evangelist at the age of ten and preached in several local churches and rescue missions until we left Los Angeles in 1949.

In later years, I would return to L.I.F.E. at Angeles Temple and take classes, even learning how to speak some Chinese in preparation for going to China someday.

In 1942, we were sitting at Angeles Temple when the news broke that Pearl Harbor had been attacked. Because of the war, and the fact that no one could travel to China or that part of the world, I had to alter my course and go back to Wisconsin with my parents and attend the University of Wisconsin in Madison. While there, I took classes in childcare and nursing but did not graduate.

My stepfather found a lot of defense work as a contractor between '41 and '45, and we traveled throughout the West—Utah, California, Arizona, and Kentucky.

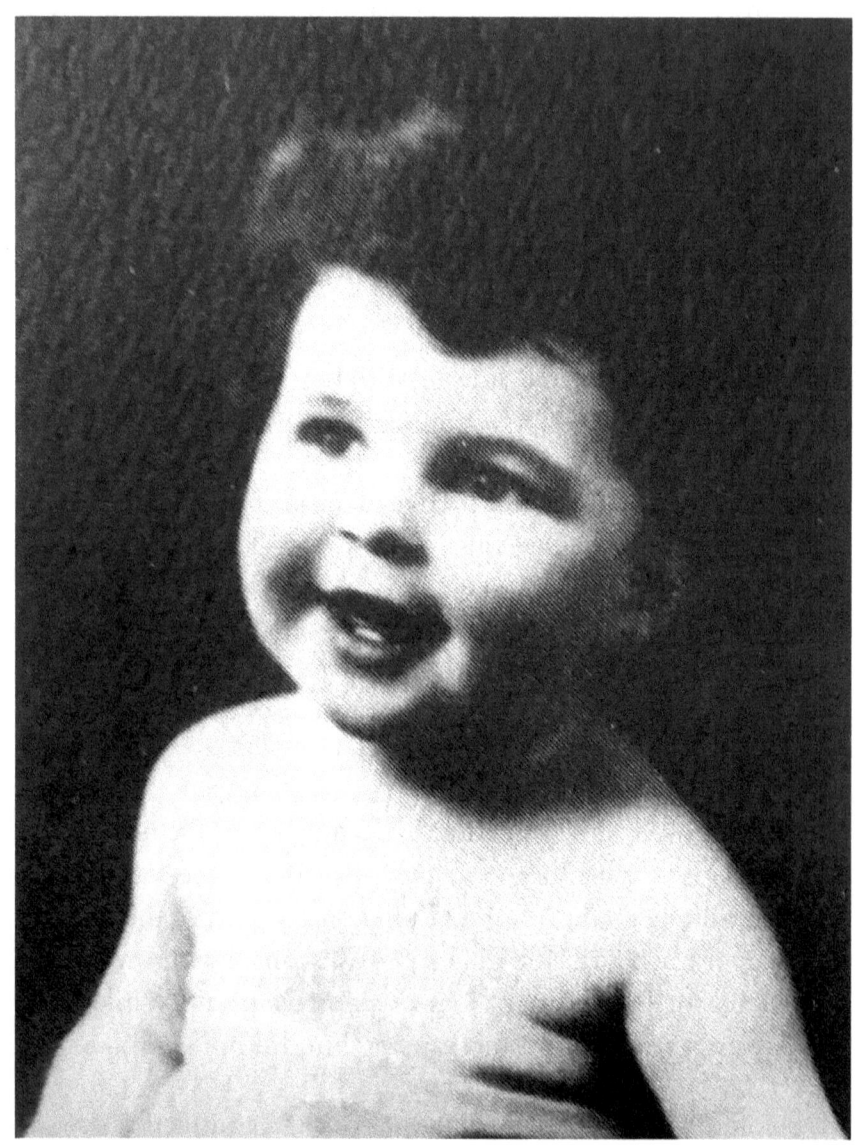

*Alyce as Ms. Baby Chicago Contest 1931*

*Alyce at age 5, Tomahawk, WI*

*Alyce as a child evangelist, Age 14*

*Alyce's father, Raymond Gabriel Davis, Orchestra Leader*

*Alyce's mother at home in Wisconsin*

# CHAPTER 2

In 1950, when I was twenty years old, I got a job in Louisville, Kentucky, caring for a doctor's new infant. While working for the doctor, I met my first husband, Paul Keller, who was a sergeant in the army at the time. We married when I was twenty years old, in 1951, and lived in various areas where he was stationed. The first was Fort Knox, Kentucky, then in Fort Mead, Maryland, after returning to America from a two-year tour of duty in Germany with the First Armored Calvary Unit.

In Nuremberg, Germany, we adopted a little infant girl at three months old. She was born in 1954. I found her in a German Lutheran Orphanage, and my heart went out to her, as she was quite ill with pneumonia. The nurse handed her to me to take home. I could hardly believe it. My husband, Paul, came to pick me up with a jeep and said, "Who is this?" I said, "She's a little one who needs our help. They sent her home with me to see if we could get some medical advice from one of our army doctor friends."

We did have a doctor friend from Paul's regiment, and he came over to our home that evening to see her and gave her a shot of penicillin. (You have to realize that at this time, the German economy did not have penicillin and many other medical things.) The baby started to improve, and after three or four days, I asked my husband if we could adopt her and he said "no." I was so attached to her by then, and I was really upset.

He wouldn't let me adopt her, and I just couldn't take her back. My husband, who was difficult to live with, had also been coming home drunk every night. Our maid, who had been taking care of her, was also was very fond of Paula. We decided together to name her Paula after my husband, Paul.

Right at this time, I had an opportunity to go to Switzerland, as we were living in Germany. I thought, if I can't have this darling baby, I'll go away for a week or so and if he takes her back, I won't have to see it. After all, I had three miscarriages within one year, and I didn't think I could ever have a child. I dearly loved this child who needed me. So, after I left for Switzerland, apparently Paul, my husband, also became fond of the baby and when I returned, he said, "You're going to take care of this baby, and we aren't taking her back to the orphanage." Of course, I was overjoyed at the fact that he wanted to keep this baby!

# CHAPTER 2

As time unfolded, we were set to come back to the United States, even though it was a year or so early. It was something called operation "Gyroscope," where one unit would come back from the army, and another one would replace them. So, he started the adoption proceedings for Paula, as we called her, after Paul. The adoption was barely ready when we had to go, by ship, back to the United States. I hadn't yet received her birth certificate, but they let us return, saying it would be mailed to us at Fort Meade, where we were to be stationed.

To baby Paula, that was a chance to really have a life. She was about one year old, or almost a year old, when we embarked on the ship, and she even started walking on the journey. It was a very rough trip though, and she and I were virtually the only people who didn't become seasick.

When arriving at Fort Meade, Maryland, we settled into a small house near the base, and I was busy caring for Paula. Paul was very busy doing a lot of gambling and drinking. He seemed too busy to spend any time with us. Things went from bad to worse at this point. To make a long story short, I had to leave him one night after he came home very drunk and wanted his gun. He threatened to shoot me and to shoot Paula.

I had felt that day that he might do something violent and I had hidden his service revolver in the woods behind our house. That night he ranted and raved, but when he finally fell into a drunken sleep, I picked up Paula from her crib, packed a small bag, and left him.

I went to the nearby highway, flagged down a bus, and went to Washington, D.C., where I found a job at the Mayflower Hotel coffee shop. I found a room for Paula and me, where the landlady took care of her while I worked.

That only lasted a week or so, and I was so afraid Paul would find us that I was a nervous wreck.

I came home one night, and Paula was so dirty; the lady had let her son watch Paula and then he tried to rape me. So I left and called my grandparents in Wisconsin, and they sent me money for a flight home.

I proceeded to live at my grandparent's home in Tomahawk, Wisconsin. My mother was traveling around the country and was not in the picture at this time.

The divorce from Paul was very complicated, and I was still very nervous. My grandmother was not well, and I was caring for Paula and my grandmother.

February 1956: at the divorce proceedings, Paul's sister, Betty, came up to Wisconsin from Ohio for the trial and asked if she could take Paula back to Ohio for a while, so that I could get back on my feet. She did not agree with her brother and was an exceptional person. So, I let Paula go back to Ohio with her and her husband.

I thought it was just temporary, or I had gotten custody of Paula in the divorce from Paul. The divorce was final on September 26, 1956.

# CHAPTER 2

It turned out that my life unfolded and I let Paula stay there. I was not settled and had to rebuild a career and a life. I kept in close touch with my sister-in-law Betty, and Paula seemed to be doing fine. She had a family—a mother, a father and two brothers. I could not offer her that.

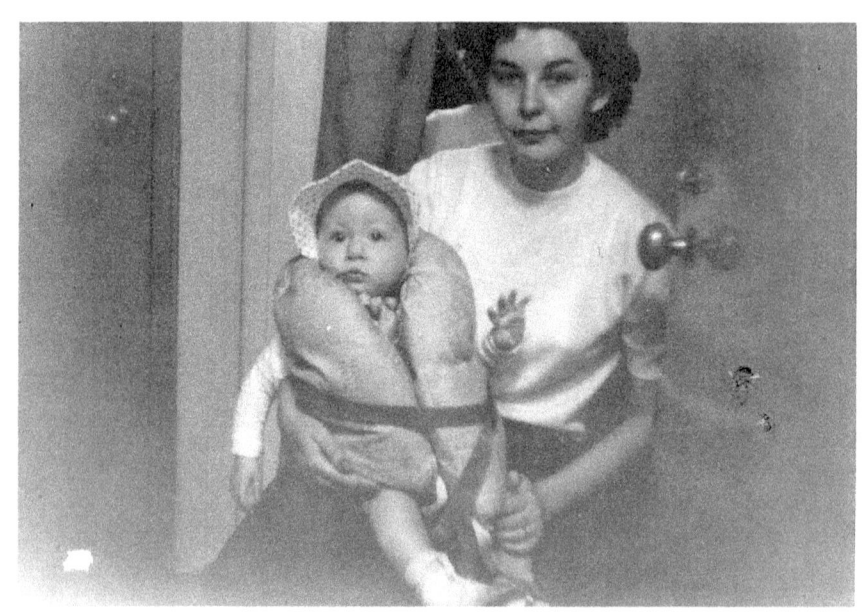

*Coming to America from Germany by ship with daughter Paula, 1955*

# CHAPTER 3

In January 1956, after the divorce from Paul and leaving my grandmother's house in Wisconsin, I went to Chicago to find a job. I began working at Compton's Pictured Encyclopedia, and I also started to take modeling and finishing courses at a local modeling school, The Nancy Simpson School. Nancy had been a Powers model in New York. I had always admired models in magazines and wanted to try my luck at modeling.

Well, after about six months, I got some modeling jobs—mostly photography for products and some fashion shows, along with fashion showroom work as well (swimsuits, furniture, etc.). I finally quit my job at the Encyclopedia and gave my modeling a chance to develop.

In late 1957, I had the good fortune of being sent to California for Norge Kelvinator Refrigerators. So, after less than a year, I moved to California, started to register with several modeling agencies, and started getting a few small jobs.

The competition in Los Angeles was very tough—all the beauty contest winners, actresses, and models from all over the world come to Los Angeles trying to make it big in entertainment or movies.

T.V. was not very big, but there were some commercials and show-biz interviews. I went to one and didn't know that it was a Las Vegas show interview. Apparently, I made an impression and was told I got the job. I then proceeded to ask what I would be doing, and they said it was a Parisian Review to be held at the Sans Souci Hotel—a hotel where the Mirage now stands!

Liberace's brother, George, was the show's producer. I asked if I wore clothes, as a lot of the shows in Vegas were going nude. They said I did, so I accepted the job.

Closing up and leaving my rented apartment in Los Angeles was quick and a great relief. No money was coming in. I started for Vegas in my old Dodge convertible with no money; I remember breaking my piggy bank for gas money for the trip! I hoped and prayed I'd make it to Vegas safely, as my car had a few rumbles and cracks, bad tires, and the front passenger door was wired shut.

The trip was uneventful except for a flat tire in the desert. A young serviceman stopped to fix the tire, and I was on my way.

The show had started as I arrived at the San Souci Hotel, so I went to the hotel desk and asked for my room key. (I also got my room and one meal a day included in the salary).

# CHAPTER 3

The desk clerk gave me a key, and I went to see the room—it looked quite small, with two single beds, and I was about to unpack when I saw a picture on the dresser of a man and his mother and a signature that read, "To Jerome, with love, Mom." I then caught a glimpse of a man's shoes under the bed.

Well, I was shocked and marched down to the desk to tell them that there must be a mistake, as the room I had been given had a man staying there. I wasn't going to accept that!

The desk clerk laughed so hard he almost cried and said, "Oh, it's only Jerome, he won't hurt you!" Well, I demanded to know who Jerome was and he told me he was the principal ballet star of the Royal Canadian Ballet, which was featured in the show. "I don't care," I replied. "I want another room."

Then he showed me to a large, back bungalow where several showgirls shared a huge room, with about ten beds, all very makeshift and **not** air-conditioned—and this was in Vegas, which can get very hot. I had the distinct feeling that I might have had better accommodations in the room with Jerome! Anyway, I settled in an empty bed area and put away some of my clothes and went to see the show.

The show was very professional. The theatre was small but elegant and the casino was charming—all in a smaller, more elegant setting than most of the big hotels in Vegas.

I worked there for a few months and was a Parisian Model in a fashion show number named "I Love Paris." It was very easy to do—a short number that I did at the beginning of the show to set a Parisian scene. Then the Royal Ballet Dancers, led by Jerome, came in and did ballet and showgirls and dancers brought up the last number, which was a spectacular finale!

After a few months, I heard from my mother, who wanted to move to Las Vegas to be near me. I told her we could get an apartment together, which we did. My mom was very religious and went to church each night, so I had to drive her there before going to work at the San Souci.

The stage manager didn't believe me and joked about it when I was late one night coming back to start the show.

A better paying job was offered to me after I joined AFTRA, the stage union, and was a member of the Union, so I could then apply for better jobs.

So, I auditioned and was hired by the Dunes Hotel as a showgirl. I had to introduce stars like Pinky Lee, Veloz and Yolanda, a famous dance duo, Lou Costello, and many others. The show at the Dunes was grand, professionally produced, and held in a very big showroom. The audience was more affluent and sophisticated, so I had to have more training as a showgirl and worked seven nights a week, three shows a night. Since mom lived with me, I didn't have any home duties; I just worked, ate, and slept. I got up at noon, ate a light brunch, and spent time at the pool, going into work at five to eat dinner, then I would put on makeup and do a show at seven, a second show at eleven, and a final show at one in the morning. I met many stars and performers while in Vegas, but I had no time for dates or social events.

## CHAPTER 3

During this period, 1956, I had many possible jobs in Los Angeles through my modeling agencies and some movie projects that seemed to be coming up. I sometimes traveled during the day for an interview and then was back to do the show the same night. I was beginning to feel that show business was not for me between the three shows a night and the fact that some of the people I met, and those I worked with were not of the caliber I wanted to become closely associated with.

I was not sorry I had the showgirl experience. However, it just didn't seem like my life's work. I also didn't look favorably on some of the people and their lifestyles. Having my mother living with me, with her religious background, kept me down to earth. I had been brought up to revere people who have faith and are honest, and I didn't find that true in some of the show people. I was looking for a chance to move back to Los Angeles.

I was off duty for two days and was so tired I slept through the first twenty-four-hour day, and when I awoke twenty-four hours later, I was starving, so I went in to pick up my check at the Dunes and have dinner.

I then went to The Sands hotel, and I sat down to hear a little of the "Rat Pack" who were performing in the lounge at the time. Sinatra, who was performing, saw me sitting there and he came in to do the show and came over to me as he walked by. He asked me where I was from and what I was doing in Vegas. I told him I was a showgirl at the Dunes and he said he was going to come to the show the next night. I didn't think too much of it.

Another showgirl I knew joined me at my table—Giselle—who was a former Miss Germany. Also sitting at the next table was a group of men who were attending a liquor convention in Las Vegas. One of the men came over to the table. His name was Arnold Frisch, and he introduced himself as being from Chicago and asked if we would like to join his table. We said "no," but he offered to buy us a drink. Giselle accepted, but I was leery of the offer.

After Giselle's drink was served, the group of men came over to our table to introduce themselves. One of the men came over to me. He said he was from Chicago and worked as an advertising account executive for Barton Distillery. He proceeded to talk about the people he knew there. In no time, he asked me for a date, but I didn't accept at first. He gave me his card—his name was Stanley D. Levitz.

The next day, I was at the hotel having my hair done when Stanley came running out of the pool to answer a page and we almost bumped into each other. He was wet and dripping on the casino rug. "Quite a specimen," I thought. When he saw me, he immediately took the opportunity to ask me for dinner and show that night.

And, so we met and our first date was at the Sahara as we watched Louis Prima and Keely Smith perform in the Lounge for the early show.

# CHAPTER 3

The next night, Sinatra came to my show with seventeen of his buddies and sat in the front row. He didn't see me until I appeared in my French outfit and walked in, doing the "I Love Paris" number. The whole party was clapping, and when I took off my gloves at the end of the show, of course, I threw them to Sinatra. He saw me in the light booth up above, when my part in the show was over, and he gestured for me to come down to his table after the finale.

At Frank's table, he asked me where I grew up. I said, "Tomahawk, Wisconsin," and he laughed and said, "You could freeze your bird off there."

Frank later asked me to join their party for dinner, but I declined. I saw one girl in their party who was very drunk and I didn't think it was a good idea to go with this group.

A few weeks later, when a girlfriend who I worked with at the Dunes was found dead in her car from an overdose of heroin, her boyfriend was arrested for her murder. I felt this situation was my cue to leave.

I continued to write to Stan after he went back to Chicago and I went back to Los Angeles. I had a small apartment in Los Angeles that happened to be in the very same apartment that Marilyn Monroe had lived in several years before on Crescent Drive in Hollywood. I continued to be a very busy model with a continual round of modeling calls and film interviews, which kept me very busy. However, I still thought of Stan, wondering if it might be possible if we could make a life together.

Stan continued to write to me and send cute cards to me, although I also did get a few phone calls in which he asked me to come back to Chicago. So, right before Christmas, my mother and I went to Chicago, where we stayed at the Allerton Hotel right on North Michigan Avenue. I saw Stan during the holidays, and then mom and I returned to Los Angeles. While I packed up my apartment and sold my car, mom went back to live in her favorite city, San Francisco.

*Glamour shot of Alyce by renowned photographer
Maurice Seymour, Chicago, 1959*

*Alyce's modeling photos, Chicago, 1968*

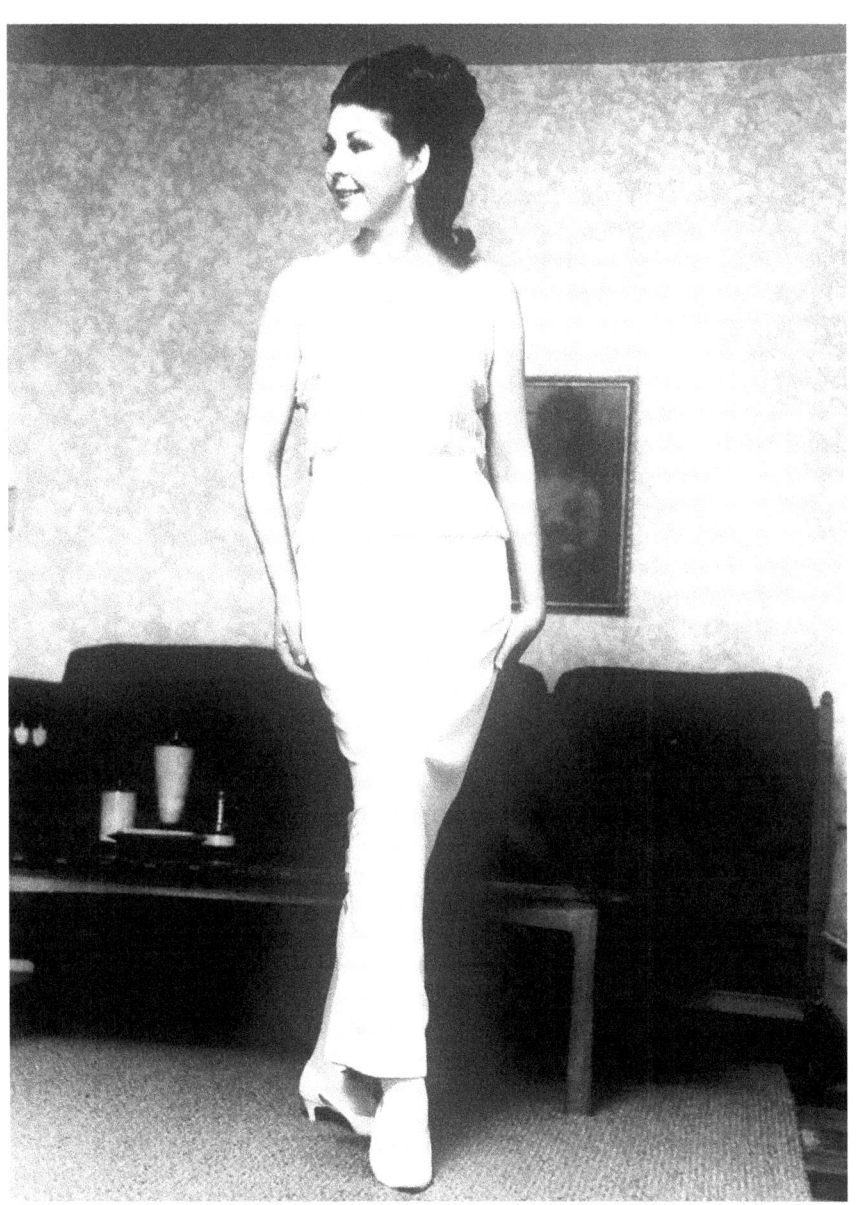

*Alyce's modeling photos, Chicago, 1968*

# CHAPTER 4

Now, I was living in Chicago again and began working at the Crane Company, which was well known internationally for its plumbing and bathroom appliances. I was the receptionist for their national headquarters on South Michigan Avenue, and I did some modeling jobs for their company. Simultaneously I had entered the modeling field again in Chicago by way of doing quite a few jobs for different trade shows as well as publicity shots for the movie industry. I did some fashion and product photography sessions as well as television commercials. My relationship with Stan was growing. I met his family, and they seemed like nice people, but they were reserved. I learned that Stan had another girlfriend, Charlene, with whom he had a date every Saturday night. Stan's family did not especially like this woman. The family was torn between Stan's girlfriend who was Jewish, and me, the showgirl and the model who the family knew was not Jewish. I guess this is why they were a little worried and feeling that our affair was getting too serious.

Finally, it was almost a year later, and I had come to feel that Stan wanted to be with me, but other things were holding him back, things like the steady girlfriend, Charlene, who was Jewish and whom he had been dating for maybe seven or eight years by then. She worked as a copywriter for an advertising company, and Stan was also working in the advertising industry. I was not aware of Charlene exactly. I only knew that Stan could not take me out at all on Saturday nights and he told me this was because he had to take clients to dinner on Saturday nights. I mostly believed him, but I did wonder whether there was another woman. Finally, one Saturday night I was having dinner and who should walk into the same restaurant?

Stan and Charlene! When they saw me, I lifted my glass in a toast to them. Stan turned pale. He very quickly hurried Charlene out of the door. The next day he called me on the phone to ask, "What were you doing there?" And, I replied, "What were *you* doing there with *her*?

Stan was not happy that I had found him out and seen Charlene first hand. Even though I still wanted to be with him, I found it in me to stand up to him and tell him I was going back to California and couldn't see him any longer. I didn't think our two worlds could come together. He was upset of course, and I spent a long night crying and couldn't sleep.

The next morning, after I got up to get ready for work, the doorbell rang. I looked through the peephole of my apartment door and saw Stan standing on the other side. He asked to come in, and I told him "no." I continued to get ready to go to work, leaving him standing in the hall. Later, when I tried to leave, he was still outside my door, this time crying, saying that he wasn't going to leave and he wanted to be with me.

# CHAPTER 4

I finally opened the door, and he walked in and started begging me to stay with him. I cried too, but I was very firm. I told him I wasn't planning to stay in Chicago when I had come to be with him and that I was planning to quit my job at Crane Company that day and leave for California by the end of the weekend.

He pulled me down beside him on the couch and proposed to me, saying he wanted to marry me and that he would never see Charlene again!

I weakened and said I'd stay for a while and think about his proposal. I really wanted to get out the door and go to work, and think about what to do about Stan, and the whole situation.

After two or three weeks of flowers arriving every day, dinners, and a lot of apologies from Stan, I decided to stay, marry him, and make my life in Chicago. Marrying Stan also meant that I would have to convert to Judaism, as his family was conservative and he felt it would be better to have me convert so that it wouldn't be a problem later on if we had children. It was not my converting to Judaism or his family that stood in the way. I did wonder because he was Jewish and I didn't know if I would be able to convert because I was a Christian all my life and my mother wanted me to be a missionary in China. However, I thought it would better to have me convert than to have a marriage that practiced two faiths. This way, we could also be married in the Jewish Temple. He and his parents wanted that, and I didn't fight them. After all, I loved Stan and wanted to please him and his family. I thought about it a long time and decided that if we ever had children, I would want them to have parents that would be of the same religion. So, I started studying Judaism and converted just before our marriage on February 20, 1960.

## TO JEFFREY WITH LOVE

We had a simple wedding at Temple Shalom on Lake Shore Drive in Chicago, and the reception was held at the Sheraton Hotel on Michigan Avenue on the West Side. Many of our friends and colleagues from the advertising agency and the Barton Distilling Company (his clients) attended a very lovely reception.

My dad was in town and had recently started working in Chicago, so he was able to film the wedding and come with his fiancé.

I made many good friends as we started our life together in a new luxury apartment building, El Lago, on Lake Michigan in Chicago. We were two of the first people to move in, and we looked right down at the lake whether it was frozen or the water was lapping at the shore.

Our life was filled with parties, friends, and my new job with the Patricia Stevens Modeling Agency. I was an instructor and counselor selling courses to young women and children who wanted to become models. I started modeling again—small photo jobs, trade shows, showrooms, runway modeling, and TV commercials. I did some commercials for Kleenex and all of the products that the Kleenex Company sponsored, like Windex and others. I also did some fashion photography for Marshall Fields, Carsons, and others.

We were trying to have a baby at the same time but it wasn't possible for us, so we began to think about adoption.

It so happened that we knew a lawyer, Larry, and his wife, Bev, and while having dinner with them one night, Larry told us of a family that had come to him to put their daughter's baby up for adoption. We said, "We'll think about it." It wasn't long after our meeting that I had another miscarriage. The doctor also told us my chances were very slim of being able to carry a baby to full term.

# CHAPTER 4

We decided to go forward with the adoption process. We checked with the doctor, and he said there was no problem with the background of the family, so we went ahead with it.

We adopted a baby that was due in late May. I took a job as "Super Woman" at the Restaurant Show as a model wearing a Super Woman costume to demonstrate cooking ranges and refrigerators. Of course, I had all the baby furniture and clothes just waiting for the baby to be born. No one expected the baby to be born earlier, but that is precisely what happened.

On the second day of the show where I was wearing the Super Woman costume, I got a phone call from my modeling agency telling me that my husband, Stan, had called from Florida where he was at a liquor convention. The doctor had called him to tell him that the baby had been born! The baby, a boy, wasn't due until May 25! We were so excited, because we had wanted a boy and, in case it was a boy, we had already picked out the name—it was Jeffrey.

Later that day, after I finished the shoot, I finally got to the hospital. Since Stan was still in Florida at the liquor convention, I wound up going to the hospital (Deaconess in Chicago), taking along a girlfriend's baby seat to take the baby home in. In those days, we didn't have cell phones, so I tried to find a pay phone to call Stan.

When I arrived at the hospital, I saw this beautiful baby boy. I just couldn't believe how darling he was. He had blue eyes, with fuzzy blond hair on his head! He seemed so small, and I noticed he had some marks on his forehead from the instruments used during his birth. The nurse said he had been a breach birth, but he did not show any problems. I never saw his mother, but I could tell that she had to have had a very tough birth. I started home with the baby in his car seat. The nurse had put a six-pack of his formula in the car and given me directions on how to mix the formula and sterilize the bottles. They wrapped him up warmly, as it was still cold. He was born May 8, 1964.

When I arrived home to the apartment at El Lago on Sheridan Road, I took him up to the apartment and immediately put him on the changing table, which we had set up, of course, in our bedroom. I wanted to look at all his little fingers and toes. I took off all his little clothes, and oh, he was such a beautiful baby. I thought, "Oh, what are we going to name you?" We still didn't have a name. Oh, my goodness, his mom suffered so much having this baby, and I had wanted one so badly. I didn't know whether to cry or laugh.

While I had him on the diaper-changing table, the phone rang, and I held him with one arm and got the telephone with the other. It was another modeling agency calling saying they had a job for me. I said, "Sorry, I just picked up the baby." "What baby?" she said and hung up on me! So, that was the end of that modeling agency. They never called me again!

# CHAPTER 4

Anyway, I went back to counting all his fingers and toes—just so perfect, a beautiful little child. I proceeded to call Stan again and finally got ahold of him, and he said, "Oh, how I wish I were there." I said, "He is cooing right now. Do you want to hear that?" So, I put him on so his dad could hear him.

I managed pretty well with him. He didn't sleep very well so there I was all alone for a couple of nights until Stan came back from Florida. He came home to us the next day. Everything was great, Stan was home, we showed the baby to his family, and we had a big baby shower. However, we still had not named him. We had thought of several different names, and finally decided that Jeffrey was the one! We felt too because of the Jewish tradition, they usually name the child after a relative—if not the first name, then the second name, David.

Somehow, we came up with the name Jeffrey David. David was for one of his grandmother's parents or something. I don't know. Anyway, there we were with a baby. A picture was taken of us when Jeffrey was seven days old. I was exhausted, but I was young then and didn't even show that I was tired and had been up all night. We were just so delighted with our baby. I stopped modeling for a while. They did call me a few more times, but I said, "No." I just had to devote myself to my child.

All of his doctor's appointments, shots, and everything went well, although he didn't sleep through the night and cried a lot. He had a little problem because he was always hungry! We had to increase his formula because it wasn't enough. He just kept crying and crying. It was a hunger cry. Then he started growing and making all the milestones. He seemed to be fine.

I didn't work through this period—I just devoted myself to my new role as a mother. I loved walking him in his buggy with other mothers and babies that lived in our building.

My birthday was on May 4, and Jeffrey was born on May 8. Since Stan was away, we decided to celebrate our birthdays after he came back from Florida. I wanted to have a party for him. We had all the family over to introduce him. I don't remember much about the party. I only have pictures of his first birthday party.

One more thing I have to mention. When I came home with Jeffrey from the hospital, I remember kneeling to pray. I was so happy to be a mother, and the fact that I couldn't have babies and the fact that his mom had given birth to this child, and was never to see him again—I wondered how she might have felt. I kneeled, prayed, and said, "Dear God, please bless this child, bless our being the parents of this child, and please comfort the mother. If there is any reason that you don't want me to have this baby, please let me know. I don't want to take this child away from the mother." So, I remember praying, "Dear Lord, bless this child; help us to be good parents." Then I went on about my business of getting him ready in his little clothes.

He had all the equipment, like a little swing and all kinds of things that we had picked up for him. He started with the right formula, the right everything, including the right doctor. Stan was bragging about him and couldn't wait until he had a little bobblehead Chicago Bear football player doll. That was going to be Jeffrey's first toy. We had a cute picture taken when he could first sit up. There were all the things we were planning for him and thinking about life insurance, etc. God had given us this beautiful baby, after the frustration about not having our own!

## CHAPTER 4

I loved walking Jeffrey in his little buggy, and I would go shopping in supermarkets and see all the other mothers. There was one mother who lived in the building, Larissa, who had a little girl named Jackie. We met her a couple of months after Jeffrey was there and they became little friends. Therefore, he had a girlfriend. Her buggy would be right next to his. We would go to the supermarket together.

When he was one year old, and not crawling, the other baby, Jackie, was already starting to walk. We thought that there might be a problem, so we took him to the doctor. Jeffrey would scoot along on his little butt to get places or he would roll. We also set up an appointment with a specialist on the Southside of Chicago, who diagnosed Jeffrey with Duchenne Muscular Dystrophy! It was such a shock. I'll never forget driving home from Chicago's Southside thinking, "My God, the doctor just told me my son has a terminal illness and how am I going to manage it?" In the following months, we took him to many specialists and doctors. He finally started to walk at three, but only after much therapy at the Rehabilitation Center of Chicago, where I became very friendly with the head doctors there, and so did Stan, who was calling all over to find out what could be done.

I started to be very active in the Muscular Dystrophy Association at that time, hoping that we could find a cure before Jeffrey was much older. However, my hopes started to get dashed when Jeffrey's doctor mentioned that sometimes children would walk for a while, and then stop. One doctor said that children with Muscular Dystrophy don't live to adulthood. I was crushed. We thought we had everything—a beautiful baby, a happy marriage, Stan's career was going well—and then this. While I had started back modeling for a bit, there would be no time for it now. I began to take Jeffrey for daily strengthening and stretching exercises so he could walk.

Eventually, Jeffrey's illness took a toll on my marriage. Although my intention when I married was to stay with Stan through thick and thin, after I discovered Stan was having an affair, and with Jeffrey's situation so involved, in the early 1970s I decided to get a divorce and move to California when I was offered a job modeling and demonstrating products for Max Factor in Los Angeles. I also became their spokesperson for their line of beauty and cosmetics.

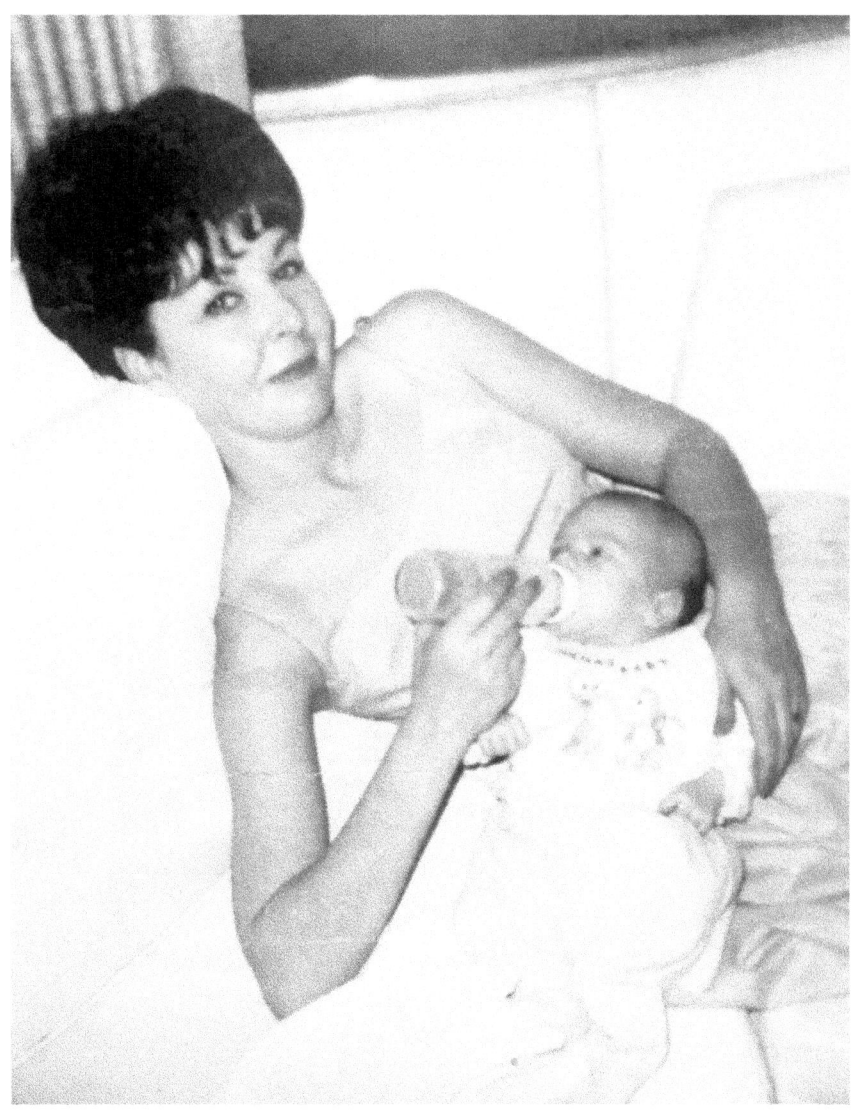

*Alyce and Jeffrey at 3 weeks old*

*Jeffrey, age 5*

# CHAPTER 5

When I arrived in Los Angeles, I discovered that the hotel Max Factor had set me up in did not allow children. Then, after I did find adequate housing, I couldn't seem to find quality childcare for Jeffrey. I was at a complete loss. I hadn't realized how difficult it would be to work and find qualified daycare. To take care of Jeffrey properly, I had to give up the job with Max Factor and wound up taking on several waitress positions and other odd jobs to pay for our room and board. I had no relatives or friends in Los Angeles and Stan had lost his job in Chicago and wasn't able to send me any support for Jeffrey.

Work was so difficult to come by, and eventually I had no choice but to go on unemployment. I was just about destitute. A man, Irving, a friend whom I had known before my marriage, whom I had started to date again, gave me a holiday gift. I thought as I began to open it (as we had affection for one another), "Oh, it's probably an engagement ring. He's going to ask me to marry him!" However, when I opened the box, it was the legal corporation papers for a nonprofit, the "Jeffrey Foundation."

"Irving, this is very nice, but what am I going to do with a Foundation?" I asked. To which Irving answered, "You'll figure it out!" "Are you asking me to marry you?" I continued. "No," he said. "I will never marry." I simply replied, "Well, you know what, Irving, it's over between us." I was so angry, thinking, "How dare he give me a Foundation to run?" Not very romantic.

The paperwork sat in my drawer for quite a while. Then one day I thought, you know, maybe I should do something with this Foundation. I had been volunteering at the Muscular Dystrophy Association and had become the volunteer chairman on several of their projects. By this time, I had managed to get a job with Jerry Lewis Cinema in Century City, and Jeffrey and I were living in the hills of Hollywood in a house we rented. I was running to work every day at Century City and putting Jeffrey in school, which did not work out too well. I started thinking about how I might do something with this Foundation.

While working at the Jerry Lewis Cinema office in Century City, during my breaks I began to make phone calls and plan a program for children like Jeffrey and their parents, to take them to the beach and do other activities, such as art programs.

I found Aaron Brothers to be very supportive and we wound up having a little art show at the Aaron Brothers Art Mart. In fact, Al Aaron was the Foundation's first donor. They provided us with art supplies as well as a teacher, Jack, who taught our children at the Junior Arts Center in Hollywood. We had children coming every Sunday with their parents for art classes. Young singers and other entertainers like David Kinnoin also came to entertain with music to keep the children occupied. Parents came and brought the whole family.

# CHAPTER 5

Most of the children had muscular dystrophy, just like Jeffrey, and were in wheelchairs. At the time, no one was paid, not even me, but we had a great group of volunteers to help us!

That was the beginning of The Jeffrey Foundation. Then, after a very wealthy lady bought one of the children's pictures of a butterfly on a tree, the purchase gave us the rent for an entire year at the Boy Scout headquarters in Mar Vista. We ended up renting the space for seven years and started to grow as an agency.

Eventually, because we didn't have the funds to purchase the Boy Scout headquarters, the building was sold to Windward School. Afterward, we moved several times and continued to operate after-school programs in the LA Unified School District.

In 1975, I married John Morris, a newspaper executive. John and I operated a group home in Mar Vista housing twelve children, Jeffrey being one of them, for over twelve years. It was a wonderful experience. However, when my husband passed away in 1989, I sold the house. Shortly after that, I found a building on Washington Boulevard that I felt would make a great center, which is where we are located to this day! Today, in addition to this building, we have two other beautiful buildings that help serve over two thousand children and their families annually.

*Back Row Left to Right: Tahitian Performer,
Diane Deshong, Mary Levin Cutler
Front Row Left to Right: Alyce, Jeffrey, Tahitian performer's child*

*Jeffrey Foundation Building*
*5470 W. Washington Boulevard*
*Los Angeles, CA 90016*

*Jeffrey Foundation Building 2019*

*Alyce and husband John Morris, wedding day, 1975*

*The Jeffrey Foundation Home children (2 images)*

# CHAPTER 6

As of May 2019, I am eighty-nine years old, and as of March 2019, I have had the Jeffrey Foundation for forty-seven years. I am still working at the Jeffrey Foundation as the board chair and Executive Director and with our Board of Directors we are carrying on the programs we started and the operation of the children's programs. We are also now planning for our 50th Anniversary in 2022.

Having a board of directors and reliable team at the Foundation gives me a chance to put my story into words, and it feels so good to be able to write about how we started and let others know how you can make a difference for special needs children and their families!

After my marriage in May 2001 to Edgar Winston, a former architect and actor, there were other life challenges. My husband, Edgar, fell in 2011 and suffered a spinal injury. I cared for him and ran the Center after a merger with another nonprofit agency that did not work out. We almost lost our Center and The Jeffrey Foundation in 2013. We continue to keep active in the community and have many friends and supporters!

A loyal board member, a parent, and many good friends helped me fight back, and now we serve 147 children a day. I work as the Executive Director and still am a part of the forty-seven-year-old organization that I founded! We will celebrate the fiftieth year of The Jeffrey Foundation in 2022.

We have served thousands of low-income children, many with special needs, and their families. My next plan is to lead the organization of Special Child USA (specialchildusa.org), a nonprofit that I founded in 1998. Special Child USA's primary purpose is to replicate the successful programs of The Jeffrey Foundation throughout the United States.

I am so proud of being able to help all of the families for all of these years and hope the Foundation will have many more years of serving special needs, low-income children, and their parents from my efforts and out of my dedication to my son Jeffrey.

## CHAPTER 6

Our national arm of The Jeffrey Foundation is Special Child USA, which will be serving other states in the United States. Through the Foundation's Development Department, I'm currently actively speaking to other organizations, individuals, and city officials about organizing programs for youth with special needs and their families in other communities. Please feel free to contact me if you're interested in learning more. Also, visit our website at www.specialchildusa.org.

Please contact us on the web at www.thejeffreyfoundation.org.

*Alyce and her husband Edgar Winston,
Wedding in Maui, May 31, 2001*

*Mrs. Sybil Brand, Event Philanthropist and Founder of Sybil Brand Institute for Women was my inspiration!*

*46th Anniversary Celebration of the Jeffrey
Foundation with Circle of Love friends*

*Left to Right: Honorable Congressmember Diane Watson,
Bunny Amber, Alyce, Larry Covin, Beverly Cohen,
Poppy Paulos, Mara New and Fred Paulos*

*Peter Mark Richman and wife Helen Richman
Peter served as MC of Foundation events and Chair
of our Celebrity Committee for 30 years!*

*Connie Stevens and little Bridget*

*Jeffrey Foundation's 46th Anniversary and High Tea and Founder's Award Reception*

*Jeffrey Foundation Board*

*Back Row, Left to Right: Dave Kinnoin (Circle of Love), Ben Blakeley (Board Member), Marcia Brickley (Board Member), Honorable Congressmember Diane Watson (Ret.), Jason Brown, Marvin Espinoza*

*Front Row Seated: Left to Right: Shana Forman (Circle of Love), Tonia Agron (Board Member), Alyce, Beverly Cohen (Circle of Love Beverly Hills Chair)*

*Alyce and California State Pre-School Students*

*The Jeffrey Foundation Staff*

*Foundation Students, Summer High School and School Age Program*

*Alyce, Spider-Man, and California State Pre-School Students*

*Circle of Love Aloha Sunday Brunch*

*Left to Right: Foundation friend Princess Karen Cantrell, Mara New (Circle of Love Event Host), Elaine DuPont (Circle of Love), Tonia Agron (Circle of Love Culver City Chair), Alyce, Poppy Paulos (Circle of Love), Maryann Ridini Spencer (Foundation PR, Marketing, Fund Development & Circle of Love), Suz Landay (Circle of Love Hancock Park Chair), Shana Forman (Circle of Love).*

# A Brief History of The Jeffrey Foundation

1971 Alyce Morris Winston's seven-year-old son, Jeffrey, suffered from muscular dystrophy.
Alyce worked with Jerry Lewis's Muscular Dystrophy Association and developed the idea of providing daycare for disabled children , as there were no centers qualified or willing to provide this much-needed service.

1972-74 Alyce founded The Jeffrey Foundation, named after her son. Activities such as camping and classes were made available to special needs children.

1975 The Foundation's first day care center opened with 25 children enrolled.

1976 Full-day vacation camps and Boy Scout Troop #75 were established.

1977 The Foundation received its first vendorization by a Regional Center.

1978 Operation Outreach provided services to the homebound handicapped.

1979 A group home for severely handicapped teenagers opened in Mar Vista.

1980 Preschool program opened. The Variety Club presented JF with a new van.
Jeffrey died of his illness.

1981 After-school program at McBride Special Ed School was established.

1982 The Foundation was receiving 40 calls a day on outreach.

1983 The Foundation was featured on nationwide television.

1984 By request, a special program opened, taking 56 severely disabled children.

1985 After-school program at Salvin School began.

1986 The Foundation's group homes were selected as model residential facilities by the State.

1987 The Foundation was serving more than 300 clients annually. Adult effective living was begun for former students who no longer fit into the school system.

1989-90 An old plumbing warehouse was purchased to become the present Childcare Center. Initial remodeling was done using Alyce's personal credit card.

1992 Social work and early intervention program began.

1993 Preschool (2-4) intervention began.

1994 18-month-olds were added to preschool.

1995 The Infant Center opened.

1996 The Parent Training Center building was leased.

1997 The 25th Anniversary of the Foundation was observed.

1999 A large grant from CDD allows purchases and remodeling of the Parent Training Center.

2001 Natural environment early intervention services stated with the help of Prop 10, CDD, and Prop K.

A BRIEF HISTORY OF THE JEFFREY FOUNDATION

2001-02 Grants allowed the construction for Administrative Office/Infant Care building and created extra classroom space to serve over 125 children daily.

2002 The 30th Anniversary of The Jeffrey Foundation, which was held Mar. 14, 2002.
In September 2002 a major remodeling project was started.

2003 Several special events were held, including a dinner honoring the memory of Steve Allen, and another honoring Carl Terzian.
Alyce received "Woman of Larchmont" Award

2004 New strategic plan, board expansion, and training launch.

2005 New approach to early childhood and after-school collaborative alliances with Los Angeles Unified School District. Focus on parent training and and family support system, with health education and collaboration with health facilities.

2006 Remodel and repair of building at 5470 W. Washington Boulevard to become Parent Child Training Center funding by Prop K and CDD green-lighted. JF receives commendation by mayor's office.
Alyce Morris Winston receives Association for Fundraising Professionals Award "Fundraising Professional of the Year."

2007 New contract signed with Los Angeles Unified School District.
Alyce Morris Winston receives Lifetime Achievement Award.

2008 Grand opening of Special Child & Family Resource Center.

2009 Five-year accreditation granted to J.F. by the National Association for the Education of Young Children; Mayor commendation awarded to JF as well as Certification of Recognition by California Legislature Assembly.

2010 Collaborating with National Inclusion Project – Special Needs and typical children learning side-by-side, promoting greater understanding.
Alyce Morris Winston recognized by LA Business Journal as Pioneer.
2011 Early Head Start, Kedren, and LA UP successful ongoing programs.
2012 Making Parenting a Pleasure awarded for one year by Department of Mental Health of County of Los Angeles.
2013 LA Housing & Community Investment Department — Early Reconveyance Loan for buildings 5470 W. Washington Blvd on October 2013.
Five-year accreditation granted to J.F.by the National Association for the Education of Young Children.
Making Parenting a Pleasure awarded for one year by Department of Health of County of Los Angeles.
Enhance all our programs: Early Start, Early Education, Pre-Kindergarten, School Age Renewed of First 5-Los Angeles Universal Pre-School.
Family Resource Center (FRC) 300+ families completed our Parenting Classes
2014 Launched Circle of Love Campaign to raise funds for our infant program to reopen on May 2014.
Spring Camp from April 14, 2014 to April 19, 2014.
Celebrating our 42nd Anniversary
2015 Alyce Morris Winston was a nominee of the Los Angeles Business Journal's Women Making a Difference Symposium & Awards on May 4, 2015 and was one of the finalists for CEO.

## A BRIEF HISTORY OF THE JEFFREY FOUNDATION

2019 The Jeffrey Foundation celebrates 47 years.
Alyce receives Los Angeles Business Journal "Trailblazer" Award at Women's Council & Awards
We're constantly developing and creating new programs to help the community.

In 2022 we celebrate 50 years!

# Alyce Morris Winston Biography

Jeffrey Foundation Founder, Board Chair and Executive Director

Alyce Morris Winston started the Jeffrey Foundation in 1972 with the desire to give her son, Jeffrey, who had muscular dystrophy, a better life. After quitting her job as a model and makeup consultant for Max Factor, Alyce began to develop a grassroots program to provide special needs children with activities and outings they could enjoy. These outings, which instilled a sense of pride and accomplishment in youths with special needs, also provided their families with much-needed companionship and support.

Today, the Foundation, located at 5470 West Washington Boulevard in Los Angeles, through high-quality programming and support services, helps both the child and the family to successfully meet the challenges posed by developmental disabilities, autism, multiple handicaps, Down's Syndrome, in utero drug exposure, crippling accidents, poverty, abuse, abandonment, and neglect. The Foundation also extends its services to typical children through its programs of inclusion and outreach so that the community may benefit from these additional resources. Parenting workshops and courses in child rearing are also offered at the Special Child and Family Resource across the street from the Foundation at 5443 West Washington Boulevard.

For her pioneering role in the social service community, Mrs. Winston is the recipient of numerous honors including: The Jeffrey Foundation Board and Parents *Lifetime Achievement Award,* 2019 "Trailblazer" Award from the Los Angeles Business Journal Women's Council & Awards, City of Los Angeles *Mayor Commendation, Certificate of Recognition* by the California Legislature Assembly, *Child Care Innovator of the Year*, California Community Foundation *Unsung Hero*, Susan B. Anthony *Professional Woman of the Year*, American Mothers Inc. *California Mother of the Year*, Sybil Brand *Humanitarian Award*, National Philanthropy Day *Founder Award*, Association of Fundraising Professionals *Outstanding Fundraiser Award*, and Children, Youth & Families *Angels Over LA Award* among others.

For those of you who wish to help special needs children or others that need help in the world, don't give up! When you think you have something that might help, go to your local schools or wherever to get some assistance and guidance! Perhaps you can call The Jeffrey Foundation, we'd be glad to work with you if you have ideas on how to help Special Needs Children and their Families. I adopted this little boy & had no idea he was handicapped or had special needs. I just thought of ways that I could help him & myself as a mother, so that I could work, and help other families as well.

So don't forget to keep on going, don't give up! Never, never, never give up! As Jeffrey used to say, "Mom, let's keep going." So that's my message. Don't let trials and tribulations stop you. Don't let having a Special Needs child stop you. Just keep on going and trying to improve the world around you. Our center and the services we have provided for 47 years is a testament to our efforts!

www.ingramcontent.com/pod-product-compliance
Lightning Source LLC
Chambersburg PA
CBHW060502110426
42738CB00055B/2596